Anxiety & Depression 101 - Everything You Need To Know!

By

UnselfishMarketer.com

Table of Contents

Chapter 1 – Introduction

Unless you have been lost at sea over the past ten years, you have probably not only heard about depression and anxiety, but also heard about them on a daily basis. You have also most likely watched countless advertisements about this that appears to be a "new disease." Depression and anxiety are nothing new. They have been good buddies that have followed some folks around since the beginning of time. It is just now we are free to talk about it.

Why are we free to talk about it now when psychiatry has been around for nearly 150 years? Probably because there is a lot of money to be made in treating these illnesses with pharmaceuticals. And pharmaceutical companies want to sell drugs that are supposed to cure depression and anxiety so that they can make money.

What are depression and anxiety? Are they diseases or just weaknesses to which certain individuals fall prey? Those who are proponents of modern psychology feel that they are diseases that must be treated with medication and therapy. Those who are against modern psychology feel that this is a state of mind that can be overcome with strong will. Who is right?

This book will teach you not only about depression and anxiety and the different levels of this disorder, but also a bit about the history of depression, the different ways that they manifest themselves, how to tell if you need treatment and many different ways to treat both disorders.

Most information that you read about depression or anxiety is created to sell you a certain cure or idea regarding these matters. Very few are objective when it comes to their reporting. Most will be slanted one way or another. If you read information from a pharmaceutical company, for example, they will tout the different medicines that are available for depression and anxiety. Then there are the all natural cures that will tell you how dangerous medication is.

Then there is this book. This is you all comprehensive book about depression and anxiety. Here you will learn everything there is to know about depression and anxiety in easy to understand language. You will also visit with some people who have suffered with depression and anxiety and see how they helped themselves. By learning all of the facts about depression and anxiety, you will be better prepared to make a decision regarding your own treatment or the treatment of a loved one.

This book is not meant to give you medical advice. Depression can be a serious issue that can require medical attention. This book is meant to help you understand a bit about depression and anxiety and what type of cures and treatments are available to you today.

Chapter 2 - What Is Depression?

Everyone gets the blues all of the time. No one is happy, happy, joy, joy all of the time unless they are on drugs.   If you are like most people, you have had days where you have felt depressed. You may feel a little weepy or feel sorry for yourself. This can be related to an incident that has happened in your life or for no particular reason. Some say that we get depressed because of the weather. There is even a mental disorder called "Seasonal Affective Disorder" that is supposed to be triggered by lack of light.

Depression is tough to define. It can be different things for different people. A person with a negative personality, for example, may seem depressing a lot more than a person who is always positive. This is why it throws you for a loop when the person who is always positive jumps off a bridge and the person who is always negative is still around. Depression is not always easy to spot and is different for each individual.

Clinical Depression is a serious illness. People who are clinically, severely depressed usually try to commit suicide at one point in their lives Sometimes they succeed. They find it difficult to maintain jobs or relationships. They tend to look at the glass half empty, which is an old cliché but rings true with those who suffer from depression.

People who are severely depressed for long period of time are diagnosed with clinical depression. This is one of the major reasons why many people are disabled in the United States. Back pain and clinical depression claim most of the disability claims in the US each year.

A person who is clinically depressed cannot "snap out of it." It can be frustrating for loved ones to watch a person in this condition as the natural instinct is to shake them and tell them to "snap out of it." We tell them how grateful they should be for everything that they have and point to people who have it far worse. We may as well be talking to a wall. The clinically depressed person cannot just decide to not be depressed one day. They realize that there are others far worse off than them, but it doesn't make them feel any better. This type of "therapy" that is often given to the depressed can do more harm than good. It makes the person who is suffering from depression feel as though he or she is being self indulgent.

Some people take it a step farther and accuse the depressed person of "seeking attention." This is also damaging to the psyche of a depressed person, particularly because depression is so closely related to self esteem issues.

Depression comes in many different forms for each individual. It will most likely manifest itself by making a person who suffers from this illness lethargic and not interested in doing every day things. The person who suffers from depression may not like to do anything. They may sleep too much or not at all. They may feel angry and lash out at people a lot of the time. They may also feel angry with themselves.

In some cases, a person will go through the motions of their every day life without no joy. They seem almost like an empty shell. They look for any type of relief from this state that they can get, which is one reason why so many people abuse drugs and alcohol.

You may or may not realize that someone is suffering from depression. A person may appear listless and not have any energy or they may put on a really good front. Two sad cases of people who had depression are Marilyn and Jimmy.

Everyone used to call Marilyn "The Grim Reaper." She was always dark and moody. She used to talk about death a lot of the time and also drank to excess. She went from doctor to doctor to try to get help for her depression.

Marilyn used to say that depression was like a dark cloud that followed her around. If you knew Marilyn, you could almost see the cloud. She walked slumped over and never seemed happy. Even after she began seeing the doctor for severe depression, she still never seemed to spruce up.

Marilyn's family said that she had been depressed most of her life. Coincidentally, Marilyn's mother had committed suicide when Marilyn was a little girl. Apparently, her mother was also clinically and severely depressed.

When she was 30 years old, Marilyn took an overdose of barbiturates that had been prescribed for anxiety and washed them down with whiskey. A friend found her body the next day after phone calls went unanswered. None of her friends or family was that shocked that Marilyn killed herself. She didn't even leave a note.

Jimmy was one of the most popular kids in high school. He was a gifted athlete who had a full scholarship to his dream college. He had a ton of friends in school and a girl who he also liked. All his life, things seemed to come easy to Jimmy. He exceeded at sports which made him well liked throughout his school career. It also made his parents very proud of him.

Jimmy's parents had just gotten divorced after a long and strained marriage. Jimmy and his sister were both upset about the divorce and missed their father who had moved out of the family house. But Jimmy appeared happy on his last day of school, the day before high school graduation.

Looking back on that day, most of his friends realized that they had been left clues. They just didn't pick up on them. That day, when Jimmy went home, he parked his car in the garage and left it running while shutting the garage door. His sister was at a friend's house. Jimmy knew she was going to be gone and that his mother was at work. He knew no one would find him until it was too late and he was right.

Jimmy left a note. It told his parents that he had been depressed for some time and that his suicide had nothing to do with the divorce. He felt that he had had a good life and, at the age of 17, felt that it was time for him to "move on."

The news of the suicide devastated Jimmy's family as well as his friends. The entire school was affected. Thousands of people went to the wake where his stunned parents sat in disbelief. His sister, who found his body, was also there. The entire family was in shock as was the school.   No one saw it coming.

The sad thing was that Jimmy's school as counselors. They have classes and seminars about depression. They have teachers that are taught how to look for "the signs." The kids have access to counseling whenever they want it. Jimmy was the fifth student to kill himself in the last four years at the school.

Depression is not always evident. There are people who walk around like Marilyn all of the time but have no intention of ever killing themselves. There are people who appear to have everything going for them and then suddenly do something drastic, like Jimmy. You can never tell.

Only the person who is experiencing depression can help themselves. Parents of a person who is depressed can take them to the doctor and the doctor may even prescribe medication, but if the young person will not take the medication, or, when they reach a certain age, refuse to take the pills, they cannot be helped. They may even, like Jimmy, realize that there is a lot of attention placed on depression and decide to hide it so that no one finds out.

Contrary to what you may think, not everyone who suffers from depression has suicidal thoughts. Most just have thoughts of emptiness and despair. They don't want to die but don't' want to live, either. They may try to get help for themselves, like Marilyn, or may deny that there is anything wrong at all with them, like Jimmy.

In short, depression has many different forms and takes on a different meaning for each person. No one is sure why some people suffer from chronic depression and others do not. Most of us, however, at one time in our lives, will deal with depression of some sort.

How you deal with depression is up to you. Hopefully, the more you realize that it is an illness that can be treated by a number of different ways, you will try to fight the depression and not give in to the dark feelings that may overpower you.

Chapter 3 - What Is Anxiety?

Whereas depression tends to make someone lethargic and not feeling like they want to do anything, anxiety makes them jumpy, nervous and in a state of fear. Anxiety is fear of the unknown. It is easy to put a name on this disorder. Anxiety disorder manifests itself in a variety of different ways. The root of anxiety, most psychiatrists believe, is depression. People who are depressed often also experience anxiety. These two disease go together like peanut butter and jelly.

Some of the ways that anxiety manifests itself include obsessive compulsive disorder, anorexia nervosa, social anxiety disorder, phobias, general anxiety disorder and others. These are all different syndromes that also manifest themselves in different ways. And they all have one thing in common - it is all about control.

People who are depressed often suffer from anxiety and vice versa. Excessive worrying is one way that obsessive compulsive disorder manifests itself. Usually a person with obsessive compulsive disorder worries about germs or the house burning down or the doors being unlocked. He or she performs rituals to give them a bit of control over this worry. The worry is usually not about the doors being unlocked or the house burning down but a fear of the unknown. People who experience this illness tend to have more problems with obsessions and compulsions during chaotic times in their life when everything is out of control.

Anxiety often triggers panic attacks, or anxiety attacks. This can make someone feel as though they are having a heart attack. They feel all of the symptoms of a heart attack and usually end up in the emergency room of the hospital. When they find that they have had an anxiety attack, they are relieved. Until the same thing happens again.

Anxiety attacks can be really dangerous. Some people actually faint during such attacks from hyperventilating. This can happen anywhere, even when driving. Others may ignore true heart attack symptoms thinking that they are having an anxiety attack. Anxiety also raises the blood pressure of most individuals. It makes a person feel as though they are crawling out of their skin.

Anorexia nervosa is actually a condition that stems from low self esteem and depression and can be considered an anxiety disorder. A person with this condition has the delusion that they are fat, even though they are rail thin. They continue to starve themselves. Singer Karen Carpenter suffered from this disease that eventually ended up killing her. After the starvation, the body can no longer take the strain and the heart gives out.

Anorexia is all about control, as are other eating disorders. A person suffering from this disorder usually feels things spinning out of control and looks for something she can control. Most of the people who suffer from anorexia are young women, college or high school aged. They usually start out a little overweight and someone makes a remark about it. This does not do much for their self esteem which is usually already fragile because they also suffer from depression. They diet a little because of the hurtful remark and lose some weight. Viola!

They are in control of something! So they continue to diet.

Most psychiatrists will say that anorexia is a separate disorder, but it has roots in anxiety and depression as well. Anxiety and depression can usually be found in anyone with a mental disorder. They are pretty much the parents of all mental health issues, but different issues are more serious than others and the anxiety and depression manifest themselves differently.

According to Dr. John Bolton of Palos Park, Illinois, depression and anxiety usually are the result of low self esteem. A person who suffers from these disorders sees themselves as worthless. The feeling of low self esteem makes them feel powerless and causes depression. The constant need for some sort of control over their environment and feeling of being powerless to help themselves causes the anxiety. They are afraid most of the time and cling to a certain fear in order to feel "safe." The fear, or phobia, is usually something that is imagined in their head and in many cases, does not even exist.

Sigmund Freud, who is considered the father of modern Psychiatry, felt that depression was the result of stifled creativity. Freud noted that many depressed individuals were also highly creative. There are those who agree with Freud's theory and those who take issue.

Today, the feeling is that people who suffer from depression have a chemical imbalance in their brains that can be "cured" with artificial serotonin that is given in pill dosage. People who have anxiety are usually treated with tranquilizers by the medical community as well as therapy. Most doctors today subscribe to the theory that people with depression and anxiety have a physical illness that is due to a chemical imbalance in their brain. They also believe there may be a genetic link.   Others disagree with this theory and believe it is the result of low self esteem or problems in childhood. Still others blame society and poverty for people feeling depressed.

In short, medical science has a lot of theories about why so many people suffer from anxiety and depression, but no clear cut answers. But there is one thing that you will rarely hear a doctor say, and that is "I don't know."

Chapter 4 - Theories About The Causes of Depression and Anxiety

As mentioned in the last chapter, there are disputes in the medical field regarding the causes of depression and anxiety. Some psychiatrists are very Freudian in their belief that this is all about stifled creativity. Others blame genetic makeup. When we talked about Marilyn, we noted that her mother also committed suicide. It appears that mental illness, such as depression and anxiety, can be inherited.

Other doctors blame society. Poverty will cause depression. Take a look at people who are living in poverty for most of their lives. Their faces reflect a blankness as if they don't care about anything. You can see it from their behavior. The drug use is rampant in poverty stricken areas, as is alcohol use. Why do people think this occurs? It is because the people who are so despondent, who are subjected to misery on a daily basis, tend to look for a quick fix and begin to self medicate. Our answer, as a society, is to arrest them for using drugs.

Some doctors actually blame drugs and alcohol for the depression and anxiety. They are few and far between, While alcohol does nothing to help those with depression and is, in itself, a depressant, it is the symptom of the disease of depression, not the cause. Alcoholics, like most addicts, suffer from low self esteem, depression and are looking for some way to control part of their environment.

Then there are those in the psychiatric field who believe the illness is physical. We have a chemical imbalance of serotonin in our brains that must be alleviated by taking medication, called SSRIs. This discovery coincides with the discovery of SSRI medication and promotion by the pharmaceutical companies. There are no medical tests that can determine if those with depression suffer from a chemical imbalance in the brain. As it stands now, this is just another theory as to why some people are prone to depression.

If you ask a priest or a religious person, they will tell you that depression and anxiety are due to a lack of faith. People who have faith in a particular religion seem to suffer less from depression and anxiety. But is the religion the reason why they do not suffer or is it their form of self medication? Just like some people get addicted to alcohol and drugs and use them as a crutch to get through life, others uses religion. This is a much less dangerous crutch to an individual, unless they become fanatical to the point where they are causing harm to others.

Some people believe we all have a degree of depression and anxiety. That anxiety is the fear of the unknown that exists in all of us. The thing we fear is death - the one thing that no one wants to face but we all must sooner or later. It can also trigger depression. Freud also said we had a death wish and a life wish. Perhaps depression is a signal of our death wish.

There are many different theories on why people become depressed and anxious. The theories will also dictate the cures or treatments. A medical doctor, for example, will be quick to prescribe drugs. A Freudian psychiatrist may be more apt to try a cognitive therapy. Therapists, hypnotists, acupuncturists, herbalists, priests, doctors and the guy at the car dealership all have different theories on depression and all have an idea of how it should be treated.   Most people in the United States, however, go to the doctor when they are feeling depressed.

Chapter 5 - How Doctors View and Treat Depression

If you go to your family doctor and complain about anxiety and depression, they will quickly whip out a prescription pad and prescribe Xanax, Wellbutrin, Zoloft, Paxil, Klonopin or a number of other drugs that are created to treat anxiety and depression. Years ago, before the terms "anxiety and depression" were coined, people were considered to be "nervous." They had "nervous breakdowns." They were treated, at best, with Valium, which is a highly addictive tranquilizer.

Today, people are no longer diagnosed as "nervous." There are dozens of different names for "anxiety disorders." Instead of Valium, they are diagnosed with Xanax or Klonopin. Both of these drugs are equally addictive tranquilizers and not that far off from Valium. All of these drugs are made to be used for short term but are usually given for long term periods. People who are "nervous" really like these pills and soon become addicted. They build up a tolerance in the system and the person taking them needs more and more to get the same results.

Years ago, strychnine was considered an appropriate treatment for nervousness. Only in small doses, however, as too much of this lethal poison might send you into violent convulsions and result in death Strychnine was prescribed as late as the 1950s for anxiety.

Prior to that, we had good old heroin that was a great remedy for nervousness. It was available in drug stores and was so effective at relieving anxiety that they decided to use it as a children's cough medicine, too.

If anyone got too lethargic after their dose of heroin for their anxiety, they could always have a little cocaine, which was also available. This was a great pick me up for most people.

Today, this almost seems comical. But we have to wonder if the drugs that are being prescribed today will also be looked upon as dangerous as those that were prescribed for these conditions even 50 years ago.

Many of the drugs we use today to combat anxiety and stress have serous side effects such as liver damage resulting from long term use. The scary thing is that we really don't know how the drugs will effect us on a long term basis because they have not been around for along period of time or tested on enough people to really make us understand what we can expect from long term use.

Depression Drugs

Anti depressants are different than anti anxiety drugs. Anti depressant drugs are usually prescribed with anti anxiety drugs but are meant to be used on a long term basis. Some doctors will tell a patient that they will need to take the drug "forever."

These drugs are called SSRIs. This stands for selective serotonin reuptake inhibitor. These drugs are meant to rebalance the lack of serotonin that is believed to be lacking in the brain of someone who is suffering from depression. Prozac was the first of these to really make a name for itself in the country. After Prozac came an entire host of antidepressant drugs. Currently, the most widely prescribed SSRI drug is Zoloft. These drugs are not only used to help with depression, but are also supposed to be helpful in treating anxiety disorders that often accompany depression.

There are side effects to using SSRI medication. They include vivid and extraordinary dreams, dizziness, weight loss or gain, inability to achieve sexual pleasure, panic attacks, and photosensitivity. You may also find that you get tremors and nausea as well as headaches when you initially start taking SSRIs. Once the drug is in your system, the side effects seem to dissipate.

One of the most troubling of the side effects of long term use is the potential for liver and kidney damage. This can be especially troublesome if a young person is diagnosed with depression and prescribed SSRIs, although this is rare as there has been a rash of young people who have commit suicide after being prescribed drugs like Paxil. For this reason, SSRIs are rarely prescribed in anyone under the age of 18.

There is a question in the medical community as to the effectiveness of these drugs. There are many critics in the medical community who do not feel that SSRIs are effective at all in treating people with depression and should never be given to people with mild depression. There are those who feel that the drugs should be reserved for extreme cases of clinical depression instead of given to people who are upset because a boyfriend or girlfriend broke up with them.

There are also some questions regarding how useful the drugs are in actually treating depression. Although they proved, in a clinical trial with the FDA, that they were better than a placebo in treating depression, there was not that much of a clinical difference.

Lawsuits have been filed due to some young people who have committed suicide after being prescribed these medications. There was also a noted lawsuit in which a man who killed 8 people with an assault rifle while on Prozac. The family of the many sued the makers of Prozac and the case was settled out of court.

There are many different types of depression drugs on the market today. If you have been diagnosed with clinical depression, your physician will most likely prescribe one of these drugs for you. You should keep a journal of your feelings on each day and be aware that it will take a couple of weeks for the drug to enter your system.

If you do not notice a difference, tell your physician. He or she will most likely prescribe a different drug or a higher dosage. Anyone with clinical depression, especially when there are thoughts of suicide, needs to be treated by a medical doctor. Serious depression is nothing to play around with. There are drugs that can help alleviate your symptoms.

Although we have talked about side effects of depression drugs and how they might not be needed in cases of mild depression or even moderate depression, people with serious depression need help. Medication, in some cases, is the answer. Although we often hear tragedy stories about people who have taken medication and done something drastic, and we all imagine the pharmaceutical companies rubbing their hands together looking to make a buck off of us, there are many, many people who have found a new lease on life by taking anti depressants. There are some cases in which these drugs do wonder for some people. It is tempting to say that those who respond well to the treatment most likely do have a chemical imbalance, most likely inherited, that the drug can correct.

Other people with mild depression who were prescribed anti depressants are very vocal speaking out against the drugs. The withdrawal from most anti depressants is anything but pleasant and many people liken with a sensation of going out of one's mind. There are scores of websites devoted to anti - anti depressant drugs. They feature forums where people tell harrowing tales of being hooked on anti depressants and how they had to get off of them.

The decision to go on anti depressants should be one that you make with your doctor. Realize that a lot of the information on the internet and that you read regarding anti depressants is either pro pharmaceutical or anti pharmaceutical. There is a movement that is against pharmaceutical companies because they are big business and assumed to be corrupt. Try to make up your own mind whether anti depressants are right for you.

If you are suffering from severe depression and have any thoughts of suicide or harming others, seek immediate medical care. There is help available for you that will immediately make you feel better.

Anxiety Drugs

Anti Anxiety drugs, unlike anti depressants, are not meant to be taken over a long term basis. They are highly addictive and are usually sedatives. They include Xanax and Klonopin to name a couple. Valium was their predecessor, but it is not widely prescribed. All can be considered tranquilizers, although this term is not used any longer. The appropriate phrase is "anti anxiety medication."

Unlike anti depressants, most anti anxiety drugs give instant relief. They have a calming effect that is very easily to get used to. Many critics of anti anxiety medication refer to them simply as "booze in a pill." This is because they tend to have the same effect as drinking only without the hangover.

Like alcohol, anti anxiety drugs are also very addictive. Very addictive. They also create a tolerance in your system, also like alcohol. You have probably heard of people building up a tolerance for alcohol. This refers to the fact that you tend to need to take more and more of the drugs in order to get the same effect. This builds up over a gradual period of time.

The trouble with taking anti anxiety drugs is the addictive quality of the drugs as well as the tolerance build up. It does not take long before someone is abusing these drugs. When a person who is addicted to tranquilizers runs out of the drug, they will resort to all sorts of means to get the drugs. This includes even going on the black market or buying them on the internet. This can be a dangerous practice, not to mention expensive.

Other ways that people get addictive anti anxiety drugs is to doctor hop. This entails going to more than one doctor and asking for prescriptions. You then take the prescriptions to various pharmacies to have them filled. You are very concerned that you do not want to run out of the prescription so you make sure that you stockpile them.

Another dangerous activity of those who are addicted to anti anxiety drugs is the habit many have of mixing alcohol with the pills.   The alcohol sometimes will enhance the effects of the pills so that they are more potent. The mixture of alcohol and barbiturates have led to more than one death.

One of the problems with mixing alcohol and pills is that you forget how many pills you took and don't realize how much alcohol you are drinking. Anti anxiety medication has an effect that is similar to alcohol. Your reflexes slow down. Your brain gets fuzzy. Your coordination is off. You are warned not to drive or operate heavy machinery when taking these drugs.

Withdrawing from the pills can give you greater anxiety than when you began. It is a paradox. You withdraw from something that is supposed to have cured you from anxiety only to get worse symptoms of anxiety than before you even started. Withdrawal from drugs such as Xanax can be like a roller coaster ride through hell and back. It is a tough habit to break.

Most doctors will advise weaning you off of the drug slowly. This is easier said than done as it requires discipline that the person who is, by now, a bona fide drug addict, does not have. You are better off to have a friend help you wean yourself off of the drugs. Going cold turkey is the worst way to rid yourself of the habit of anti anxiety medications, but once they are out of your system, you should begin to lose the anxious feeling.

Being addicted to anxiety medication can almost be as bad as having anxiety. In this case, the cure is sometimes worse than the disease.

Chapter 6 - Therapy To Treat Depression

If you visit your family doctor and ask for something to help you over your depression, he or she will most likely give you Zoloft.. They will ask you why you are depressed and you can say that you didn't like the outcome of the last season of American Idol and they will write you out a prescription.

Doctor's take a lot of heat for being prescription handy. But they are only doing the job that the legal field has trained them to do. See, if you go into the doctor's office and complain about being depressed over American Idol and the doctor tells you to get a grip on yourself and dismisses you without a prescription and you go home and hang yourself because of American Idol, the doctor is liable for a lawsuit. Because medical protocol requires a doctor to offer medication to any patient who presents complaining of depression.

If your doctor is a good family doctor, he or she will suggest that you speak to a therapist about your depression. He or she may also want to get you out of their office as soon as possible and suggest that you see a psychiatrist. Your doctor is not telling you this because he or she thinks you are crazy and need to be committed, but simply because he or she does not specialize in mental health issues.

Before we go any further, you need to understand the difference between a psychiatrist, a psychologist, a counselor and a therapist.

A psychiatrist is a medical doctor. He goes to medical school and has an M.D. He then decides to specialize in mental illness. A psychiatrist normally works in a hospital. He takes care of patients in mental wards as well as those who have substance abuse problems.

The main reason why a person sees a psychiatrist is to get prescription drugs. Because he is a medical doctor, he can prescribe drugs. The idea of laying on a sofa talking about your mother while the psychiatrist takes notes is something that you see in the movies. A psychiatrist is very clinical. He may test you for diseases of the mind, but will not want to hear how your brother taking your stuffed bunny when you were seven ruined your life.   He will refer you to a counselor.

A psychologist is a step above a therapist. He or she usually has a PhD in psychology. He or she did not go to medical school but graduate school. Big difference is that they cannot prescribe medicine. They are very in tune with mental health issues, however, and make great counselors. The problem is that they charge too much money. Most people opt for counselors.

Psychologists do a lot of court appointed work and work with children. It is unlikely that you will be referred to see a psychologist to talk about problems with your mother.

A therapist usually has a master's degree in psychology. He or she can help you overcome your issues in whatever way he or she learned. There are many different types of therapists and each of them practice different therapy. Some of them are devotees to Dr. Freud. Others think Freud was a crock. You have to shop around for the right therapist that will offer you treatment that will adhere to your lifestyle.

A therapist will most likely come up with a treatment plan to help you. They will want to see you regularly and you can talk to them about everything - it is all confidential.

A therapist cannot prescribe drugs. They can, however, refer you to a psychiatrist for medication.

A counselor is a lot like a therapist only they usually have a bachelor's degree. Some counselors, however, who specialize in such therapies as child development, do have a master's degree. A counselor mostly listens to your problems and allows you to see your own mistakes. They will do a lot of "what do you think about that" and "how do you feel about when he does that." A counselor is an unbiased friend to whom you can tell anything.

There is another person who you can see and that is an analyst. This is a person who will tell you everything that is wrong with you and why. They fall into the same category as the counselor except they are a bit more abrupt and speak their mind instead of allowing you to solve your own issues.

Your treatment will depend on the extent of your depression and anxiety. Most people can see a psychiatrist once in a while for drugs and a counselor to talk over their problems. Some will want therapy so that they can learn ways to deal with their problems without drugs. Again, everyone is different when it comes to their needs of treatment. Take a look around and see what type of therapy or treatment is right for you.

Chapter 7 - Therapy Methods For Anxiety

It is tough to treat depression with treatment. Talking about problems can get a person to unleash their problems that are disturbing them, but if you think that a few counseling sessions are going to cause someone to make a life altering revelation and reveal all of the problems of the past, you have watched "The Prince Of Tides" one too many times.

For the most part, there are behavior therapies that are taught in therapy sessions that can teach you how to cope with depression and treat anxiety. Your therapist may give you the following ideas on how to cope with anxiety:

Write down the fear that you are having on a piece of paper. This makes the fear real, and not just a figment of your imagination. Read it and toss the fear in to the trash can. This is symbolic and an attempt to toss away your fears.

A more effective method is to allow you to face your fears. Take the example of Linda.

Linda was a 38 year old mother of two who was worried about breast cancer.   A friend of hers had breast cancer she became convinced that she, too, probably had the disease. Instead of having her fears alleviated by going to the doctor, she decided to dwell on it. The worry took its toll on Linda, her job and her family.

After about three months of nearly constant worrying, Linda's body could not take it anymore and she collapsed at work. Actually, Linda had a panic attack which caused her to feel dizzy and actually faint. The fact that she was not eating properly didn't help. She was rushed to the hospital where she uttered her anxious fears. Although her physical tests came back fine, she was urged to admit herself to the psych ward so that they could help her.

In the psych ward, Linda had to undergo group counseling as well as meet with a psychiatrist. The psychiatrist ordered a mammogram for Linda and told her that she had to face this fear. She was trembling so bad when she had the mammogram that a nurse had to hold her hand. Finally, it was all over. The mammogram came back normal. Linda felt like a new person.

She stayed in the psych ward for three days and found out that perhaps the fact a good friend was facing a devastating illness forced Linda to confront her own mortality and the fact that she didn't have enough money put aside for her kids, if something happened to her. She used the breast cancer as a cover for the real worry, which was her concern for her children if something happened to her.

In addition to learning to break down her anxiety and try to get to the root of the real problem, which was fear of the unknown, Linda also faced one of her greatest fears. Now she was no longer afraid of the mammogram. She goes every year for this potentially life saving test.

Therapy really helped Linda with her anxiety. Drugs might have masked the anxiety disorder by getting her to relax, but she really needed to get to the root of the problem.

The root of the problem of most people with anxiety is fear of the unknown. Fear of death, fear of losing their job, fear of what it going to happen in the future. Although we should be wise enough to realize that there is no guarantee for the future and that anything can happen on any given day, the idea that our lives are not totally under our control scares the living daylights out most people. So what do they do to gain control? They desperately look for some way that they can control their environment.

When we think of someone trying to control their environment, we might imagine someone who is either what is termed a "control freak" or someone with obsessive compulsive disorder who has to have everything in a certain order in their home. We often refer to people as anal retentive if they have to have things a specific way to keep them from freaking out. Just about everyone suffers, to a degree, of anxiety. Everyone fears the unknown. How we deal with the issue is what puts some people on anti anxiety medication and others in the church or the bar.

A good percentage of people with anxiety drink. This is an easy way to self medicate and relieve the anxiety. It does not cure the anxiety, it is just a mask. Like tranquilizers, booze can just make a person feel calm for a moment but is not a cure. In fact, it can be downright destructive.

Taking a drink at a social occasion is one thing. Having to have a drink because you are anxious and using booze as medication is another. When combined with sleeping pills or anxiety medication, it can be deadly.

Alcoholism has long since been recognized as a disease. Alcoholics Anonymous is a very effective support group that has helped millions of people get and stay sober over the years. Just about everyone is familiar with the prayer recited at the end of the meetings. "Give me the strength to change what I can change and accept what I cannot change."

This gets right to the root of the problem that most alcoholics have. They are no different than anyone else suffering from anxiety and depression except that they are choosing a different method of medication. And long before there were tranquilizers, there was booze. People have been self medicating themselves for ions. Alcohol is the drug of choice when it comes to treating anxiety.

Alcoholics anonymous uses support and therapy to keep people sober. Drugs are not used as a replacement for the booze. The secret is to go to the meetings and continue getting the support of their fellow alcoholics. This is simple therapy. It is not performed by a therapist or counselor or anyone licensed in this field. It is performed by other people who have also been through the same problem and give their support to others so that they, too, can become sober and overcome their addiction to alcohol.

There is a line in the film "Crocodile Dundee" in which Paul Hogan's character is confused because he is introduced to someone who is seeing a "shrink." He immediately assumes that she must be insane.

Coming from the outback in Australia to New York City, his character felt that anyone who had to resort to psychiatry was, in his words, a "lunatic."

When it is explained to him that the woman was not crazy but just saw a therapist to talk over her problems, his response was "doesn't she have any mates?"

And the answer was that "we can all use more mates."

Freud went to his grave with one secret - that a psychiatrist was really just a paid friend. Most of us give more credit to the profession of counseling and therapy than that. While we do pay them to listen to our problems, unlike a friend who will always be on our side and is biased, a counselor will sometimes tell us things that we do not want to hear.

Therapy is much more effective at treating anxiety. Instead of just treating the problem with pills or self medicating with booze, we need to seek out treatment however we have to find it. Whether it is a support group, a friend or a counselor, we need to be able to let out our fears and not let them take over our lives. Otherwise, we are simply masking the problem with medication and booze.

If you suffer from anxiety, instead of reaching for the tranquilizers, reach for the phone and make an appointment to see a counselor. Most will work on a sliding scale where you can pay what you can afford. If you are in dire straits, call your local municipality and find out if there is a program that gives treatment for those suffering from anxiety disorders.

You are far from alone. There are millions of people who are already on medication and being treated for this disease. If you want to know how many are not being treated but are self medicated, take a look at your local tavern. Chances are you will find several people in the tavern who have been there awhile and are treating their anxiety with alcohol.

Chapter 8 - Symptoms

The symptoms for depression and anxiety are something that most of us will experience at one point in our lives. They are very vague and general symptoms. There are different levels of anxiety and depression and they symptoms all relate to those levels.

Whether or not we need care to deal with the symptoms depends on the severity of the symptoms and the cause. Some obvious factors cause depression and anxiety. The condition is usually alleviated when the stressor is removed.

Some people experience short term anxiety and depression upon a major stressor in their life, even if it is a happy occasion. Any sort of change can upset tranquility in a person's world. People feel comfortable with routine and a break in routine can bring about anxiety or depression. This, again, is short lived until the person gets comfortable and settled into the new routine.

If, however, the symptoms are severe that the person does not want to get out of bed in the morning, is having suicidal thoughts or is experiencing depression or anxiety for more than a few weeks, it is time to seek treatment.

Symptoms of depression include:

- Insomnia or over sleeping
- Loss of appetite or over eating
- Low or no sex drive

- Loss of interest in anything that they once took pleasure in
- Crying
- Letting their appearance go
- Apathy and just not caring about life
- A feeling of hopelessness

Severe depression would include suicidal thoughts. Many people who experience depression exhibit one of all of these signs. If everyone who ever had a bout of depression went on medication, the entire nation truly would be a Prozac nation. Most of the time, these symptoms gradually dissipate. If they persist, a person should seek treatment.

Suicidal thoughts should never be ignored, even if you believe that the person is "faking it" just to get attention. You never want to be wrong on a call like that, so you are better off to be safe than sorry.   If a friend or loved one threatens suicide, don't mess around - call 911.

Chronic depression lasts for more than a few weeks. It may be alleviated with medication. It may come and go.

Depression that is triggered by an event, such as the loss of a loved one or even the loss of a job, will usually resolve on its own. If it persists, chances are that it triggered something that was already there.

Symptoms of Anxiety include:

- Nervousness and jumpy

- Trouble sleeping - often has insomnia
- Trouble focusing thoughts
- May develop compulsive habits to keep order
- Tremors (in some cases)
- Can exhibit some destructive behavior (almost a mania in some cases)
- Excessive worrying that is not logical

Anxiety is all about a need to control an environment that is out of control. Again, it is usually triggered by depression. A situation occurs that causes a person to become depressed. The body fights the situation with anxiety. Anxiety, the fear of the unknown, wishes to control the situation so that it cannot happen again.

Having anxiety and depression is very common. Getting treated for these syndromes does not make you "crazy." If so, the entire country would be considered crazy. Millions are on medication for these illnesses as it is and millions more are self medicating with booze and illegal drugs.

While medications and therapy have proven to be effective in helping people who suffer from anxiety and depression, there are some things that they can do to actually help themselves. These natural means of treating their condition can work wonders.

Chapter 9 - Helping Yourself Treat Anxiety And Depression

This is in no way to insinuate that someone who is suffering from severe anxiety or depression can be cured by taking a herbal supplement or performing exercises or yoga. This book cannot state enough that serious depression is a disease, a serious disease that can prove fatal. A person should not treat themselves for severe depression any more than they should try to remove their own gallbladder.

That being said, in the same respect, every single person who feels a little down should not have to run to the doctor and get tranquilizers and anti depressants. There are certain things that people can do to stave off both depression and anxiety on their own. Here are some tips on how to deal with depression and anxiety on your own. Even if you are under medication, you can use these methods to help you cope with depression and anxiety.

Routine

Establish a routine of some sort for yourself.   Remember that anxiety comes from the fear of the unknown and loss of control and depression has its roots in low self esteem. A routine is a safe harbor in an unsafe world. A routine, even if it is as simple as watching a television show every night, gives you some sense of security in your life. You know that no matter how bad things get, you will still have that routine in which to rely upon.

A woman named Sarah tells a funny story about when she gave birth to her first child. Every night, she watched a specific program on television that gave her a sense of security. She was anxious about the impending birth of her first child as any new mother usually is. She was also excited about the birth as she and her husband got the nursery ready for the new baby.

Each night, she watched her favorite program on television and it gave her a sense of routine. No matter how nervous she was about the birth, she knew that she had something to look forward to each night that gave her a sense of security. In short, she had a routine.

When her baby was born, things were naturally chaotic. Her baby was a healthy little boy and Sarah was over the moon about him. But it was scary taking care of him. She was now a mother who was responsible for a life. She was happy to be a mother and loved her baby, but was very anxious.

She stopped watching her favorite program because things seemed so turned around in the house. A week after the birth, she managed to put the television on and there it was - her favorite show. And she sat down and watched.

Sarah soon began to again look forward to this program. She experienced an upheaval in her life and relied on routine to get her through this anxious time. The best part of this story is that Sarah realized how important some sort of routine can be to the mental state and also passed this on to her son and then later, her daughter. Today, Sarah's children are grown and mentally healthy. Sarah, by the way, no longer watches that particular program. She does, however, continue to rely on routine as a way to alleviate anxiety.

Exercise

Any doctor worth his or her salt will tell you to exercise if you have depression or anxiety. Again, this can be used in conjunction with medication, if medication is needed. Exercise not only helps you physically, but also mentally.   Exercise naturally raises your serotonin levels and gives you an energy boost as well. When you are depressed, however, the toughest thing to do is to exercise. It will work to help with your depression if you can just get into the habit.

Even if you just manage to take a walk or do some stretches, get yourself in to an exercise routine. This is valuable information for anyone, but particularly anyone who wants to alleviate depression. This is not to say that you cannot still take medication, but exercise can work well with the medication.

Exercise not only helps with depression, but anxiety as well. Performing exercise puts you in control of your environment, which can alleviate anxiety. Remember that lack of control makes us feel anxious so you can gain some control in your life in a positive manner if you exercise.

Some people with anxiety and depression find themselves becoming addicted to exercise. You will find them at the gym all of the time and they usually appear to be in excellent physical shape. Although addiction in any form is bad, even to something as positive as exercise, spending all of your time in the gym is better than spending it at a bar. You just want to make sure that you do not neglect other duties in your quest to stay fit.

Exercise is good for you physically and mentally. It will raise your energy level, boost your metabolism and even your immune system. On top of that, it will help you get into good physical shape. Most people who are depressed care very little about their physical appearance. Exercise helps them get into shape and gives them something to strive for, especially if they need to lose weight.

This is the cure all for a lot of different ailments, including anxiety and depression. If you are experiencing anxiety or depression on a small scale, start jogging or exercising before you reach for pills. You will be pleasantly surprised at the amazing effects.

Yoga and Meditation

Yoga is an ancient Eastern art that uses body poses and contortions to give inner peace. Meditation is also practiced in Yoga. You should keep in mind that you do not have to contort your body into impossible positions in order to achieve the benefits of Yoga. You also do not have to chant in order to meditate. Both of these ancient philosophies rely on cleansing the body and the spirit through self discipline.

You can easily learn yoga by renting a video or DVD or even reading a book. Yoga classes are available just about anywhere, even at your local park department. Meditation can be practiced anywhere. You just need about five minutes of peace and quiet and a chance to clear your mind. Think of happy, peaceful thoughts and then rid your body of negative energy. Meditation is, in itself, an art form but one that can really work to help you over tough times in your life. Yoga and Meditation are both used as methods of treating anxiety and depression as well as other ailments.

Eat A Healthy Diet

Many in the medical community believe that people who suffer from depression and anxiety have a deficiency in vitamins. You should not only eat a healthy diet that is rich in B vitamins (such as dark colored vegetables and fruits) but also Omega Fatty Acid which is found in fish. You should also take a multivitamin to make sure that you are getting all of the nutrients that you need. You may notice a change in your moods right away if you take a multi vitamin. Make sure that the vitamin that you take contains Omega 3 Fatty Acids.

Eating a healthy diet is good for anyone. Staying away from simple carbohydrates will not only benefit you mentally, but physically as well. This is not to say that you cannot have ice cream or sweets once in a while. Actually, dark chocolate is beneficial to your health and can be a mood enhancer all unto itself. But you should limit your portions of these foods and make sure that you get a healthy allotment of the foods that are beneficial to your health. Your new healthy diet will not only benefit you mentally, but physically as well.

Drink Water

Skip the soda and alcohol and drink plenty of water. You should also limit your caffeine intake. Have your morning coffee or tea, but switch to water during the day. Drinking water will not only help you maintain a healthy weight, but it will also boost your metabolism. Water is a natural energizer. While some say drinking eight glasses of water a day for health is a myth, most doctors will agree that water is very beneficial to your health.

Drinking water will also flush out your system and keep your immune system working properly. You will notice that you will fight off colds easier by drinking more water. Instead of sweet drinks, which are really only liquid candy and offer no nutritional value whatsoever, drink water.

Limit Alcohol and Don't Smoke

Although some people who are anxious say that they smoke to "calm their nerves," smoking actually increases your blood pressure and constricts your blood vessels. Smoking will make you wired, just like caffeine, so it hardly "calms you down." In fact, you might find yourself significantly more relaxed after you have kicked the habit.

Alcohol is okay in a social setting and a glass of red wine can be very beneficial to your health. Like anything else, alcohol is fine in moderation. But if you are using alcohol to "cure" your anxiety, you are making a big mistake. While taking a "stiff drink" when you have a certain problem will not make you an alcoholic or even really harm you, if you learn this behavior and take a stiff drink every time something goes wrong in your life, you are headed for trouble. Alcohol should be used only socially and never as a medication.

Socialize

Human beings are social animals. We all need human contact. It is probably no coincidence that the number of people with anxiety and depression has risen so steadily as we have become more insular. Now, with the internet, many people are working from home and not interacting with other human beings at all. While the idea of going to work in your living room in your pajamas is pleasing, it can also be depressing if you never get a chance to meet or talk to other people.

There are plenty of groups and clubs that you can join that will give you a chance to interact with other people. Find something that you like to do and join a club. Go to your local library and join a book club. Take a look at classes at your local community college or park department. Do not rely on the internet as your sole source of socialization. We all need human interaction to avoid becoming depressed.

Get Creative!

Depression does tend to plague creative people more than others. Do something creative to stave off depression. Whether it is writing, painting, singing or even dancing, use your talents and enjoy your creativity. Even if you use your time to decorate your house, you can not only have some fun doing something that you enjoy, but also keep depression and anxiety at bay.

Get Busy

If you do not know what to do, clean something. Pick a closet in your home and clean it out. This will help you deal with your anxiety and also get something done at the same time. Being active is the best way to treat anxiety and depression. You have to force yourself to do this, but once you start, you will notice a difference. Chances are that you will start concentrating less on your anxiety and depression and more on the closet or bathroom that you are cleaning. And when you are finished, you will feel good about yourself.

Depression has its roots in low self esteem. In order to build up your self esteem, try the tips outlined in this chapter. You can also use affirmations on a daily basis. Try to banish negative thoughts from your mind and keep looking at everything in a positive light.   This will help you treat depression and anxiety.

All of the ideas in this chapter are safe to do even if you are using medication. You should consult with your doctor before starting a strenuous exercise program, however. These ideas are all tried and true ways that you can treat your own depression. If you get into the habit of using all of them, chances are that you may be able to treat your depression and anxiety without drugs.

Chapter 10 - Alternative Medicine

Some people will tell you never to take medication for anxiety or depression and will recommend alternative medicine. This includes herbal remedies, acupuncture, massage and aromatherapy to name a few. Doctors will tell you that these do not work and proponents of holistic medicine will tell you that the pharmaceutical companies are running our lives.

How you treat depression is eventually up to you. You should understand, though, that most alternative medicine to treat anxiety and depression is used in cases where the condition is mild. Again, people with severe depression or anxiety, to the point that it is threatening their lives or the lives of others, should not hesitate to seek medical attention.

For those with mild cases of anxiety or depression, you can try the following remedies:

<u>Herbal Remedies</u>

St. John's Wort is probably the most popular of all of the herbal remedies used to treat depression and anxiety. St. John's Wort is effective at combating mild depression and anxiety in a natural way. It has been used for centuries in this regard and works very well. You can purchase St. John's Wort online or in health food stores. It comes in a capsule and in various different strengths.

There has been some controversy about whether St. John's Wort can cause liver damage. There have been no conductive studies on this ancient herbal remedy that indicate that it is harmful or that it can actually help with depression and anxiety. Most medical doctors will dismiss it as a crock while herbalists will swear by it. Many people have found this herbal remedy to be very useful in treating their mild depression and anxiety.

You should not take St. John's Wort if you are using any medication to combat depression as it can have an adverse affect. St. John's Wort should only be used in cases of mild to moderate depression and anxiety.

Other herbal remedies that work to reduce stress include Chamomile and Valerian.

<u>Acupuncture</u>

Acupuncture is an ancient healing art that pinpoints pressure points and uses needles to cure pain as well as treat a variety of other different types of ailments and mild conditions. There are some who swear by acupuncture as an effective pain relief as well as a relief for anxiety. The treatment sounds dreadful, but it is actually very relaxing. Best of all, you will feel as though you are doing something good for yourself by giving yourself some empowerment over your health.

There is no medical evidence for or against acupuncture in treating anxiety and depression. This method of treatment has been used for thousands of years as a cure for a variety of different ailments and is still used today, so there must be something to it. It will not hurt you to try acupuncture, even if you are on medication for anxiety and depression.

<u>Massage Therapy</u>

The need for massage has doubled in the past ten years and as a result, massage therapy has become a big business. Years ago, people conjured up the image of a sleazy red light massage parlor when they thought about massage therapy. Today, however, this is a respected profession and one that has proven to be very beneficial in pain management. There are many different professional athletes who have a full time massage therapist on staff.

Massage therapy will certainly not hurt you. To the contrary, it will feel really good and relaxing. You should treat yourself to massage therapy whether or not you have anxiety as it will relieve tension and stress. While massage therapy certainly works wonders to relieve physical anxiety and tension, it will not work to relieve the thought process that is usually generated by anxiety. For this reason, massage therapy works almost like a tranquilizer. It is a lot more expensive, but a lot less harmful.

<u>Aromatherapy</u>

Aromatherapy is another Eastern healing art that has been around for centuries. This is based on using essential oils that are derived from herbs, barks, flowers, fruits or other organic matters and either massaging them into the skin or inhaling them.

In order for aromatherapy to actually work, you have to make sure that you are using pure essential oils. There are hundreds of products on the market today that advertise to be "aromatherapy" that use synthetic products. They are not true aromatherapy. True aromatherapy uses 100 percent pure essential oils.

Some essential oils are actually toxic and should never be used. Others are photo toxic. Most should never be used directly on the skin as they can cause severe reactions. Lavender is one of the few essential oils that is actually safe to use on the skin and is one that is often used to treat anxiety and depression. You can use lavender as a massage oil or put it into an infuser and inhale the fragrance.

The concept of aromatherapy is that the fragrance will be absorbed into the bloodstream either through the skin or the lungs and begin healing. Aromatherapy has been around for thousands of years and can be very relaxing. It is usually practiced in a salon by someone who is familiar with the art form.

Aromatherapy can also be practiced in the home if you have an infuser. There seems to be a huge draw towards natural healing products and aromatherapy is becoming a popular choice in the alternative healing market.   Doctors will dismiss this idea as a crock, but again, it has been around for thousands of years and is still widely used, especially in the East. There might be something to this healing art.

You can try alternative healing methods but remember that they offer no guarantee and should only be used in cases of mild to moderate anxiety and depression. They are generally safe to use and all, with the exception of herbal remedies, are safe to use when you are taking medication. They can end up costing you a lot of money, so make sure that you trust the person who is performing the services.

Chapter 11 - The Future Of Depression And Anxiety Treatments

As people become more insular than ever and the internet continues to take control of our lives, we can probably depend on more cases of anxiety and depression. Life is not getting any easier and appears to be more complicated with each passing decade. On top of that, human beings who are used to being social, are kept alone a lot of the time. In this respect, we are almost like dogs. Dogs will get depressed if they are kept away from the pack for a long period of time.

Think about the changes that have taken place over the past couple of decades. Years ago, an office had a large pool of people in the center, mostly typists. There were offices surrounding the large typing pool, but for the most part, everyone was lumped together working.

Take a look at offices today. Look at the cubicles. They insulate everyone from one another. Is this healthy?

Years ago, before television, people would get together on Saturday nights with the neighbors and play cards. Who does that today? Who has the time? Most people would rather spend time in their homes watching television.

Even children who used to be shooed out to play years ago are now being kept inside either by choice or because parents are scared to allow their children outside. We continue to hear about children who were outside unsupervised who ended up getting kidnapped or killed.

Treatments for anxiety, depression or any mental illness has also changed. Remember the old "Bob Newhart Show?" Newhart starred as a psychologist who used to treat a group of people. He often had "group therapy." Is there such a thing as "group therapy" anymore? Or have the HIPAA laws changed that?

Do people go to church anymore? Years ago, church attendance was up. People not only went to church on Sunday, but they often socialized afterwards. Today, church attendance is way down. People do not go to church and those who do, often do not stay to socialize.

Years ago, families lived within blocks of one another. They visited each other on weekends. Children knew their cousins, aunts, uncles and other relatives. There was a family bond.

Today? Families rarely get together like that anymore. Everyone is too busy. Weekends are reserved for doing work around the house or taking the kids to one of there many structured activities.

In order to help our society overcome depression and anxiety, we will have to get back to basics. For the most part, we will have to realize that human beings are meant to be social. They are meant to have friends, family and other people around them. They are not meant to be drugged into compliance. People are going to have to start eating healthy, exercising and socializing. People will also have to stop reaching for the instant cure and trying to help themselves overcome burdens and struggles in life without always relying on medication.

Group therapy is something that should return when it comes to therapy for depression and anxiety. People also need to slow down and take some time for themselves. Make time for creative pursuits and enjoy life instead of always chasing the dollar.

The future of depression and anxiety can either be a boom for the pharmaceutical companies or it start to waver off. This is up to people who have a choice on whether they want to continue living their lives as they are now so doing and taking pills to get though the day, or if they want to slow down, take a breath and enjoy what life has to offer.

One Final Thought

In 1929, the stock market crashed that sent the country into a depression that we have not seen since and hopefully will never see again. Millions of people lost their jobs. This was at a time when most people rented apartments and few owned houses. There were no government subsidiaries to help the poor. The depression lasted for a long time. And alcohol was illegal. You could not go to the local bar and drown your sorrows, although most people knew where to get a drink if they needed one. They just couldn't afford it. Then World War II broke out.

During WWII, a good portion of the able bodied men went off to war and some never returned. Women entered the work force out of need because someone had to run the plants while the men were at war. There was rationing. You had to have coupons during the war to get gas or cigarettes (at a time when everyone smoked). You could not get nylon stockings or butter and meat was also rationed. People responded to this by growing fruits and vegetables in "victory gardens."

Many of the people who lived through the depression and WWII are still alive today. Ask them what they took to make it through their anxiety and depression during these times.

Warmest regards,
Jaykay Bak & Bren O'Hara
UnselfishMarketer.com